LUDOVICUS II.
BAVARIAE REX.
MDCCCLXV.

Neuschwanstein Castle

Between 1869 and 1886 King Ludwig II. of Bavaria had Neuschwanstein castle built on the Swan Rock, high above the beautiful Alpsee and close to the thundering waters of the 45 meter high Pöllat Gorge. The castle was designed by Eduard Riedel, the stage-painter Christian Jank and the architect Georg Dollmann. With its pointed towers, tall and slender, Neuschwanstein is a fantasy realized in stone. On May 13th 1868, the 23 year old King wrote to Wagner: "I intend to rebuild the old castle ruins of Hohenschwangau by the Pöllat Gorge in the genuine style of the old German knightly fortresses . . . the spot is one of the most beautiful that one could ever find."

The 5-story castle, built in Romanesque style using the Wartburg castle as a model, is, with its many scenes from Wagner's stage-world, the embodiment of a romantic, medieval castle.

Lohengrin and Tannhäuser, the Song Contest (in the Wartburg), Parzival's Grail and many other heros and sages of the German middle ages come miraculously to life on the walls of Neuschwanstein.

On 9th June 1886 a State Commission travelled to Hohenschwangau to remove the King. 3 days later, King Ludwig II made his last journey from Neuschwanstein to Castle Berg. On 13th June, Ludwig was found drowned under mysterious circumstances in the Starnberger Lake.

Entrance Hall to the Royal Apartments

Scenes from the oldest version of the Siegfried saga decorate the walls of the Entrance Hall. In the painting on the right wall – Siegfried forges the mighty sword.

The marble arch leads to the throne room.

Throne-Room

The Throne-Room was created as the Grail-Hall of Parsifal. It was designed in elaborate Byzantine style by Eduard Ille and Julius Hofmann.

Inspired by the Hagia Sophia in Constantinople (now Istanbul), the 2-story Throne Room with its series of pillars of immitation porphyry and lapis lazuli, was completed in the year of the King's death, 1886.

Set in a half-domed, golden alcove, the throne platform is appoached by a flight of white, carrara marble steps. The throne itself, designed in gold and ivory, was never made. The platform is flanked by paintings of the 12 Apostles, and behind the platform is a pattern of golden lions, the symbol of Bavaria.

Under the blazing sun and stars of the bright blue firmament is a painting of the enthroned Christ with Maria and John on either side. Below them, six holy kings: Stephen of Hungary; Henry VI, King of

Germany and Holy Roman Emperor; Casimir of Poland; Louis IX of France (St. Louis); Edward of England (the Confessor); and Ferdinand of Spain.

In the foreground hangs a magnificent chandelier of gilt brass in the form of a Byzantine crown with 96 candles and weighing 18 cwt.

The mosaic floor, realized by Dermota of Vienna, depicts animals and plants of different kinds.

Tower garret

The tower garret to the west of the throne room offers a magnificent view over the Bavarian landscape of mountains and lakes. Between the wooded hills around Hohenschwangau Castle (the seat of the earlier Lords of Schwangau) lies the deep blue Alpsee Lake. Behind the lake, the great chains of the Füssen and Tannheimer mountains.

On the Alpsee Lake, during a visit of Richard Wagner to Hohenschwangau, King Ludwig had the arrival of the Swan Knight Lohengrin staged under a spectacular fireworks display.

Dining Room

The Dining Room of carved oak is decorated with paintings by Ferdinand von Piloty and Josef Aigner. They present figures from the "Minnesinger" period and scenes from the Wartburg Castle at the time of the legendary Song Contest in 1207.

Over the door to the right is Wolfram von Eschenbach, the author of "Parzival" and "Lohengrin". Above the servants' door to the left is Gottfried von Straßburg who wrote the love-drama "Tristan and Isolde".

The interior design of the room is by Julius Hofmann. The table sculpture, over 1 meter high, shows Siegfried fighting the dragon – a gift from Munich artists to Ludwig II.

Bedroom

In contrast to the other rooms, the Bedroom is sumptuously carved in the Neo-Gothic style. 14 woodcarvers are said to have worked 4 1/2 years to create this room. The Monarch's bed is crowned by the most intricate woodcarving and covered with richly embroidered draperies. The wall paintings illustrate the "Tristan and Isolde" story, a story which, in Wagner's operatic realization, had deeply impressed the 20 year old King. The opera received its first performance in Munich in 1865 in Ludwig's presence.

Above the washstand – Tristan and Isolde in the garden of Cornwall Castle. Above the bed to the right – Tristan's departure from Isolde. A stream above the castle brings flowing water directly to the washstand.

The windows of the balcony give a superb view of the wild Pöllat Gorge with ist 45 m high waterfall.

Chapel

Adjoining the bedroom is the small Chapel, dedicated to the Patron Saint of the King – Louis IX of France (St. Louis). The richly carved winged-altar is set into the decorated wall, and the altar paintings show scenes from the life of St. Louis.

The stained glass windows to the right show St. Louis receiving the last sacraments. The windows are the work of the "Mayerischen" Court Art-Studio.

Dressing Room

The Dressing Room is completed in relatively simple oak panelling, and the trellis-work painted on the ceiling gives the impression of the room opening to the sky.

The wall paintings illustrate the life and work of Walther von der Vogelweide and Hans Sachs – after the "Siegfried" motives of the Entrance Hall, and the "Tristan" motives of the Bedroom, this room is given over to the world of the "Mastersinger" period.

The paintings were carried out by Eduard Ille, a student of Moritz von Schwind.

Above the wash-table with majolika articles by Villeroy and Boch, we see Walther singing at the court of the Duke of Welf. To the left, a representation of Walther's famous poem "Under the Linden Tree . . ."

The King's jewel-box stands on the small table.

Living Room

The richly decorated Living Room with its extension chamber, the so-called "Swan's Corner", is completely dedicated to the legend of the Swan Knight Lohengrin – a saga of great meaning and importance for Ludwig II.

The large murals by Hauschild and von Heckel depict "The Miracle of the Grail" and "The Arrival of Lohengrin in Antwerp".

The motive of the swan appears everywhere – on the carved and painted panellings of the walls and ceilings and in the golden needle-point of the silk upholstery and draperies. Ludwig II, who as a young prince was so overwhelmed by Wagner's opera Lohengrin that he considered it a form of enlightenment, identified himself wholly with the Swan Knight, and enjoyed dressing up as Lohengrin. The tragedy of Lohengrin was his essential loneliness. This was also the fate of the king.

Study

The Gothic-styled Study of the King is stamped with references to the history of the Wartburg Castle.

The paintings, set in finely carved wall panels, are carried out on Gobelin canvas by Josef Aigner and illustrate the Tannhäuser saga and the Song Contest of the Wartburg.

To the right of the arched doorway Tannhäuser is seen kneeling at the feet of Pope Urban IV. The painting above the castle-styled cabinet (formally used to hold the plans for Neuschwanstein) shows Tannhäuser in the Hörselberg in the arms of Venus.

Continuing the idea of the Hörselberg, an artificial stalactite cave leads from the study to the Living Room. The grotto was designed by A. Dirigl, designer of the larger grotto in Linderhof. Attached to the grotto is a small winter-garden with large windows giving a beautiful view over the plain.

Singers' Hall

The Singers' Hall occupies the entire 4th floor of the castle and is a copy of the Minstrels Hall of the Wartburg Castle in Thuringia, designed by Julius Hofmann.

The murals in the hall and in the corridor (mostly the work of von Spieß and Piloty) depict scenes from the "Parzival" saga of the middle -ages, which were, to a certain extent, incorporated by Wagner in his Sacred Festival-Drama Parsifal.

Neuschwanstein Castle, created by Ludwig as a Grail Castle and simultaneously a Castle of the Swan Knight Lohengrin, embraces yet another hero in this hall, namely Tannhäuser.

Kitchen

The completely intact Kitchen shows how modern technology was allowed to take its place within the atmosphere of the middle ages captured in the upper stories. The elaborate equipment includes hot and cold running water, and automatic spit roasters.

Marienbrücke

The romantic landscape of the castles surroundings can be fully appreciated looking from the bottom of the Pöllat Gorge up to the 92 m Marienbrücke, a cantilever bridge spanning the 45 m high waterfall.

The bridge, originally of wood, was named after Ludwig's mother, Queen Marie, a Prussian princess. In 1866 the present iron construction replaced the wooden bridge.

Hohenschwangau Castle

Standing on a wooded hill between two beautiful lakes – the Alpsee Lake and the Swan Lake, Hohenschwangau was originally the seat of the Lords of Schwangau in the 12th century.

Ludwig's father, Maximilian II, bought the ruins as Crown Prince in 1832 and had them rebuilt and romantically decorated by the designer and stage-painter Domenik Quaglio in the style of the middle ages.

Ludwig II spent a large part of his childhood and youth in Hohenschwangau Castle. It was here that he first came into contact with the saga of the Swan Knight Lohengrin, through the murals by Michael Neher and Lorenz Quaglio, and, like his father, he came to feel a close bond to the Knights of Schwangau and their history.

The first floor of Hohenschwangau Castle, with the Entrance Hall, the Chapel, the

Hall of the Swan Knight, the Schyren Room, Bertha Room and Burgfrauen Room, was occupied by Queen Marie, the mother of Ludwig II.

In the Hall of the Swan Knight, which served as the Dining Room, we see the murals of the Lohengrin saga which made such an impression to the young Ludwig.

In 1865 the King entertained Richard Wagner as a guest in Hohenschwangau Castle.

The second floor of the castle consists of the apartments of King Maximilian II and the two princes. Here we find the **Heros'- or Knights' Hall, the Welf Room,** the Authari Room, the Study, the Hohenstaufen Room and the Bedroom. These rooms were later occupied by King Ludwig II.

The Tasso Room

Formally the Bedroom of King Maximilian II, the Tasso Room is decorated with illustrations of Torquato Tasso's "The History of Rinaldo and Armida", painted after designs of Moritz von Schwind.

Linderhof Castle

In the middle of an austere mountain landscape and in the isolation of the Graswang valley, Ludwig II had Linderhof Castle built. The idea was conceived after a visit to Versailles in 1867 and Ludwig purchased the land around Linderhof, where his father Maximilian II already owned a hunting lodge, the "Königshäuschen".

Under the direction of his architect Georg Dollmann, the seclusive King had the castle created between 1870 – 1878 as a tribute to the Absolute Monarchy enjoyed by the French kings. The castle was built in an elaborate Rococo style recalling the period of the Burbon Kings. This was not a showpiece for the world, but rather a private villa, where Ludwig could retire in peace and seclusion.

Linderhof was the only building project Ludwig II saw completed, and it remained his favourite residence until his tragic death in 1886.

The main fassade of the "Royal Villa", with terraces and pool. In the middle of the pool is a gilded group of Flora and her nymphs, from the centre of which sprouts a fountain which reaches a height of 80 feet.

Entrance Hall

In the centre of the hall surrounded by red marble pillars, stands a statue of Louis XIV of France astride a horse. This is a copy of the statue by François Girardon from the Place de Vendôme.

The motto of the Burbons' "Nec Pluribus Impar" (not less than any) appears over an allegorical head at the centre of the ceiling's blazing sun. This is Ludwig's tribute to the Burbon kings, whose family line he could link with his own, as his Grandfather (and Godfather) Ludwig I was the Godson of Louis XVI of France. Ludwig II liked to identify himself with Louis XIV, and considered himself the spiritual successor to the Sun King.

West Gobelin Room

The magnificent private chambers arrange themselves in a rhythmical, colorful and contrasting succession of horse shoe and oval forms.

The West Gobelin Room, also called the Music Room, is dominated by especially colorful paintings and period furniture. The wall paintings set into gilded frames to resemble Gobelin tapestries were painted by H. von Pechmann. The period furniture is, however, a creation of the Paris Gobelin Factory. Both describe crowd and pastoral scenes from the Rococo period. Next to the richly ornamented musical instrument, a peculiar combination of piano and harmonium and curiosity of the 19th century, stands a lifesize painted porcelain peacock from Sèvres, a duplicate of which stands in The East Gobelin Room. Both the proud but shy peacock and the swan were the king's favourite animals.

Audience Chamber

Proceeding through the intimate Yellow Cabinett, completely decorated in silver, the visitor arrives in the Audience Chamber designed in 1870 by the scene painter, Christian Jank. Dominating this richly paneled oval room is the king's writing table, symmetrically flanked by two fire places of Bardiglio marble upon which stand the equestrian statuettes of Louis XV and Louis XVI. Upon the table sits a gilded writing set and gilt bronze clock.

The writing table is framed and crowned by a silk and gold embroidered canopy in green, said to be part of the coronation robe of King Otto of Greece.

The paintings over the doors and on the wall with window show alligorical scenes of the different seasons. The Lunette paintings under the gold stucco vaulting portray scenes from the french court. The two green malachite tables are a gift to Ludwig II from Czarina Alexandra of Russia.

Bed Chamber

On the northside of the castle, opening directly onto the Cascade waterfall, is the central room of the castle, the royal Bed Chamber. This room was designed by the scene painter Angelo Quaglio, was enlarged in 1884 by Julius Hofmann, becoming the largest room of the castle. The room was modeled after the "Reichen Zimmer" in the Munich Residence, in a royal blue motif, formerly lit by a crystal, candelabra with 108 candles. The marble sculptures, stucco doors and ceiling paintings present scenes from ancient mythology. Painted on the ceiling, over the bed niche, is the "Allegory of the morning" representing the sun chariot of Apollo by Ludwig Lesker. The embroidery of the silk canopy except for the needlepoint work of the Bavarian coat-of-arms remained incompleted.

Rose Chamber

Connected to the Bed Chamber is the Rose Chamber formally used as the royal dressing Chamber. It is one of the four Cabinetts which, because of their narrow horeshoe form and pastel tones, contrast sharply with the larger chambers to which they connect. The pastel drawings by Albert Gräfle set in elegant rococo paneling represent personalities from 18th century french court life, including the portrait of the mistress of Louis XV, Madame Dubarry.

Dining room

Opening into a pleasant oval, in bright red, is the Dining Room. In the middle of the room decorated with a center piece of deliciate Meissen Porcelain flowers stands the dining table called "The self setting table", which could be raised and lowered from the kitchen below, allowing the shy king to remain undisturbed during his meal times.

Both the many-limbed candelabra, as well as the holder with flowers of the centerpiece, were created by the Meissen porcelain factory.

The original drawings for the paintings done in the style of the baroque illustrators were concieved by Christian Jank, 1870–1872.

Through the open doors at either end of the room portraits in the Rose and Blue Cabinetts are visible.

Eastern Tapestry Room

Figures and scenes from Greek mythology feature in the pictures of the Eastern Tapestry Room. The group of figures, by Theobald Bechler, representing the Three Graces is reflected above the marble chimney piece. In the ceiling painting by W. Hauschild, Apollo and Aurora spread their rays over wall paintings by H. von Pechmann and projecting gold stucco work.

Hall of Mirrors

Corresponding to the Bedroom to the north, the largest and most elaborate room to the south of the palace is the Hall of Mirrors.

The popular motive of the mirror room, found so often in German Castles of the 18th century, reaches its most elaborate form in Linderhof, designed by Jean de la Paix in 1874.

The large mirrors framed in white and gold conjure up an endless corridor of crystal and ivory chandeliers. The large window opposite is also flanked by mirrors and from the couch Ludwig could enjoy the spectacle of the infinite reflections.

North Slope with Cascade Waterfall

Rising directly at the rear of the castle from a strictly formal flower bed shaped in the form of the Bourbon's "Fleur-de-lys" is the north slope. Starting from a rotunda that tops the slope and corresponds to the Venus temple on the south side, emerges the Cascade Waterfall which tumbles down marble steps before ending in a pool with fountain dominated by a statue of Neptune.

The Park

The mountainous nature of the Graswang valley strongly influence the nature and contours of the park at Linderhof.

The park, covering over 198 acres, with its terraces done in the Renaissance style and its parterres done in the Baroque style and encluding an extensive English Garden, are the creation of Karl von Effner, creating an ideal park combination of forest and mountain tranquility of exceptional beauty.

Eastern Flower Beds

Lofty beech espaliers hem the delicate arrangements in the little French garden. Johann Nepomuk Hauttmann set the scene, accenting the group of Venus and Adonis in the centre of the flower bed with statues of the Elements along the paths.

The charming figure forming the fountain with a gilded Amor about to shoot his love dart, was modelled by Michael Wagmüller.

Western Flower Beds

Low flower beds, interspersed with box-tree pyramids, lead into an oval of shady covered walks and pavillons.

In the quatrefoil of the pool the gilded figure of Fama, cast in zinc by Franz Walker, spreads her wings. She is flanked by stone figures, allegories of the Four Seasons, created by Johann Nepomuk Hauttmann.

The magnificent majolica vase with a crown of angels is the work of the Nymphenburg Porcellain Manufactury, based on the original designs of the Choisy-le-Roi Manufactury near Paris.

The **Southern Terrassed Hill,** originally conceived by the King as a Rococo
Theatre, is crowned by a classical rotunda with a marble statue of Venus within
by J. N. Hauttmann.
On the right of the picture: The 300 year
old linden tree which gives the castle its
name. The land was originally a farm
owned by the Ettal Monastery.

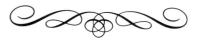

Hunding's Hut

Hundings's Hut, reconstructed in the Park of Linderhof, is a stage setting placed in nature.

Here Ludwig II could enter the world of the 1st day of Richard Wagner's Festival-Drama "The Ring of the Nibelungen", and re-live the dramatic and passionate action of the 1st Act of "Die Walküre", which received its first performance in the presence of the King in Munich in 1870.

According to Wagner's drama, Hunding's Hut, of roughly hewed wood, is built around the stem of a great ash-tree, and it is in this hut that Siegmund, escaping from his enemies, meets Sieglinde, and the "Wälsung" Siegfried is conceived.

The hut, originally built in 1876, is modeled on Christian Jank's stage-design for the Munich premier of the opera.

Moorish Kiosk

Part of the charm of the park comes from the exotic structures Ludwig had constructed there. Ludwig II had a special interest in for oriental things. Having earlier erected an indian pavillion in the winter gardens of the Munich Residence, he purchased in 1876 the already existing "Moorish Kiosk" from the castle Zbiro in Bohemia, had it renovated and enlarged and a year later erected on a hill in the park of Linderhof castle.

Inside the Moorish Kiosk

In the twilight of stain glass windows and colorful lamps, the splendid illusion of an exotic interior is created. In the curve of the apse stands the peacock throne created for the king by Le Blanc-Granger in Paris in 1877. This silk covered divan is crowned on the arms and backrest by three colorful enameled wrought iron peacocks, the fans of which are formed from polished Bohemish glass.

A moorish fountain, lanterns, smoking and coffee tables complete the scene, to create an enchanted atmosphere for midnight banquets with the king, surrounded by his entourage all dressed in oriental costumes, smoking his "chibuk", a persian water pipe. For such moonlight celebrations the king also decorated his mountain castle, "Schachen" in a moorish motif.

Venus Grotto

The Venus Grotto, one of the sculptured creations of August Dirigl was erected in 1876–1877 completely with artifical stalactite and stalagmite.

Passing through an "open sesame" stone door, opened by a secret latch, the visitor arrives in a magically lit cavern world. King Ludwig II, who from his childhood remained enchanted by the operas and sagas of Richard Wagner, recreated in the Venus Grotto the fantasy scenery of the Venusberg Mountain from Richard Wagner's opera "Tannhäuser". The painting by August Heckel portrays Tannhäuser in Hörselberg.

Underwater lighting, artificially produced waves, lighting effects created by rotating colored glass disks powered by one of the first generators – modern technology functioning in the background – help to complete the illusions of this royal dream world.

Night time sleigh rides

Just as splendid and fairtale-like as his buildings, was the life style of the king. Ludwig was particularly fond of night time sleigh rides. R. Wenig in 1880 captured one of these nocturnal outings in the vicinity of Linderhof in a painting which depicts the king in his pompous golden sleigh accompanied by rider and coachmen complete, in the style of the rococo, with white and blue livery, three cornered hats and wigs.

Herrenchiemsee Castle

In the wonderful landscape of the alpine foreland, approximately 8o km from Munich, King Ludwig II of Bavaria had his final and most costly building project realized on a 230 hectare island in Chiemsee Lake – Herrenchiemsee Castle.

In a period of increasing lonliness and isolation, Ludwig sought yet another retreat from his duties as monarch and purchased the island Herrenwörth in 1873 where he decided to erect a "New Versailles" – a tribute to the Sun King (Louis XIV of France) whose palace in Versailles Ludwig had visited and studied.

With Herrenchiemsee Castle – his Versailles – Ludwig II wanted to build a monument in honour of the absolute monarchy enjoyed by the French Kings. "It shall be a temple," he wrote, "where I can celebrate the memory of Louis XIV."

The foundation stone was laid on 21 May 1878. The architect was Georg Dollmann,

who was responsible also for Linderhof Palace. Within 3 years the construction was more or less completed. In 1884, Ludwig inspected the castle and park by night, everything floodlit by electric light. Only once did Ludwig have the pleasure of staying in his Versailles, and then for just 9 days.

The castle is incomplete, but intentinally so, since Ludwig wished only to make certain room habitable.

Two years after the king's death, the castle and its grounds were opened to the public. Ferries bring countless visitors to the island each year. From the steep shore of the island with a magnificent view of the Alps, the path winds its way through the woods to reach the castle.

Church of the Holy Cross

Situated in the heart of the Chiemgau country, Chiemsee Lake – often called the Bavarian Sea on account of its size – is one of the most beautiful areas of Bavaria. Walking paths affording wonderful views of the surrounding landscape criss-cross the terrain. The lakeside "Church of the Holy Cross" from 1697 is a reminder of the ancient village- and monastery-life of the area. Due to the surrounding oak forests the church was originally called the "Church of the Oaks".

Latona Fountain

Carl von Effner's original plan for the park of Herrenchiemsee, which was to resemble a baroque garden complimenting the island's landscape, could only be partly realized. Linden trees line the paths leading east and west to the shores of the lake, giving the grounds their symmetry. Directly in front of the great steps is a stylized french garden with immaculately pruned lawns. In the side alcoves of the lawns stand the beautiful marble fountains with figures of Diana and Venus together, and Amphitrite and Flora, created by Johann Nepomuk Hauttmann.

In the centre stands the magnificent, newly reconstructed Latona Fountain, designed by Hauttmann after the fountain in Versailles, named after Leto, the mother of Apollo and Artemis. The frogs, tortoises and fish were originally gold-plated.

Entrance Hall

The visitor enters the castle from the garden and is greeted in the entrance hall by an impressive peacock of blue-enamelled bronze – the work of Thierry and Breul. The royal bird recalls the Burbon kings of France, who were known for their interest in the orient.

Stairway

The magnificent stairway is a copy of the famous stairway in Versailles, designed for the Sun King by François d'Orbay in 1752. Ludwig II wanted more than just a mere copy – he wished to re-create the spirit of the period. Beneath a large glass roof the richly ornamented stairway with its paintings and statues is illuminated by a flood of natural light.

The walls are of marble, and the figures of Diana and 2 nymphs in the marble fountain were modeled in the studio of Philippe Perron. The paintings are by Franz Widnmann and Ludwig Lesker. The sparkling chandeliers were made by the Vienese firm Lobmeyer.

First Antechamber

The rooms of Herrenchiemsee are divided into the state appartments and the private appartments. The style of Louis XIV continues from the stairway into the grandiose state appartments, designed by Georg Dollmann and Franz Widnmann.

In true Versailles design, the series of rooms begins with a guard room, the Hartschiersaal, in which the halberds of the king's bodyguards are kept.

The first room is full of paintings in white and gold from the period of Louis XIV. Beneath the ceiling painting by W. Hauschild of the gods Bachus and Ceres in triumph, stands a beautiful Boulle cabinet decorated in tortise-shell and gold.

Second Antechamber

In the Second Antechamber the Sun King is also the dominant figure. The bronze figure of Louis XIV on his favourite horse was made by Philippe Perron. The oval windows are the same as those in the "Salon de l'Oeil-de-Boeuf" in Versailles.

State Bedroom

The real heart of Herrenchiemsee is without doubt the State Bedroom which is laid out in an almost overwhelming opulence, in homage to Louis XIV, whose bedroom in Versaille was a place where only the elect could enter to do duty to the divine majesty.

The State Bedroom in Herrenchiemsee actually manages to outdo the grandeur and opulence of Versailles. The focal point of the room is the enormous cano-py bed (3 x 2.60 m). The priceless drapes for the royal bed were ordered before even the foundation stone of the castle was laid. The bedspread alone sup-posedly took 7 years to complete and was worked on by 30 embroideress.

The scenes of Venus and Amor on the canopy were embroidered by Dora and Mathilde Jörres. The bedstand and posts were carved by Philippe Perron. The overall design of the bed was created by Julius Hofmann.

Conference Hall

Adjoining the bedroom to the north is the Conference Hall. Above the carved gold and white panelling is a ceiling painting "The Gods of Olympus" by Eduard Schwoiser.

Louis XIV is again present, with scenes from the French court and, above all, the large portrait of Louis by Jules Jury, after a painting by Hyacinthe Rigaud. The Burbon "Fleurs de Lys" decorate the draperies.

Astronomical Clock

The Astronomical Clock with the Earth, the Sun, the Moon and the signs of the Zodiac is part of a group of historical clocks that Ludwig II ordered from the Munich watchmaker Carl Schweitzer.

Great Gallery of Mirrors

The famous Gallery of Mirrors runs along almost the entire west side of the castle, joining the Hall of War at one end and the Hall of Peace at the other. Designed by Georg Dollmann this is much more than just a copy of the "Galerie des Glaces" of Versailles – it includes 17 large arched windows which allow for a continually changing play of light, and on summer weekends when chamber music is played in the hall lit by 2 000 candles, the effect is unforgettable.

Hall of Peace – Hall of War

Both the Hall of war and the Hall of Peace were modeled on the Versailles rooms, and decorated with large allegorical figures representing Peace and War. These figures were the work of Julius Frank, Josef Munsch and Wilhelm Rögge.

Private Bedroom

In contrast to the State Appartments, the Private Apartments, on the upper floor of the north wing, are in the more intimate rococo style of Louis XV, designed by Julius Hofmann an Franz Paul Stulberger.

Ludwig's favourite colour, blue, is the dominant colour of the bedroom. A special blue lamp was created by Otto Stoger, the man responsible for the lighting effects of Linderhof's Venus Grotto, which suffused the room in an eerie, magical, blue light.

The richly ornamented bed is decorated with scenes of Venus and Adonis. The embroidery of the canopy "Louis XIV trimphs over Vice" was realized by the Jörres sisters. The toilet articles are of Meissen porcelain.

Study

The Study is also dominated by Louis XV of France, with paintings of court life and a large portrait of the monarch by Jules Jury copied from a work by Jan van Loo. Even Louis' famous roll-top writing-table, made between 1760–1769 by Oeben and Riesener and now in the Louvre, was the model for Ludwig's desk which was also made in Paris. The green drapes are embroidered with delicate gold thread. The vases are a special design of the Sèvres porcelain factory.

The Blue Salon

This room was created by Drollinger and Stulberger as a morror-room decorated in the opulent Rococo style. The sweeping arabesques of the inlaid floor are continued in the branching stucco-artwork of the wall which frame the mirrors in a most extravagant way. The drapes are of blue silk, embroidered with golden thread. The fireplace of Meissen porcelain, the white marble figure of Jupiter and the white chandelier compliment the intense blue of the drapes and upholstery.

Porcelain Room

This room is decorated with the most beautiful Meissen porcelain imaginable. The original intention was to decorate all the wall panels with porcelain, but by 1886 only the door panels had been completed and painted. The console tables, multi-armed candelabras and vases are all of porcelain, as is the large mirror frame with its garlands of flowers and fruits.

One of the porcelain paintings shows an enthroned female figure with 2 putti (angels). It represents the concept of History. One putto is wearing a medaillon with a portrait of Ludwig II. It is the only picture of the monarch in Herrenchiemsee, and was placed there after the king's death.

Dining Room

The Dining Room is a large, oval-shaped room. It was modeled after a Rococo Salon of the Soubise Hotel in Paris, and contains busts of illustrious figures of the 18th century court namely Louis XV, his mistress the Marquise de Pompadour, the Dutchess of Maintenon, the Dutchess of Lavallière and the Counness Dubarry. The printings of Franz Widnmann illustrate the story of Amor and Psyche. As in Linderhof, the dining room contains a "Tischlein-deck-dich" – a self-setting table, which sinks through the floor to the kitchen below. This allowed the shy king to dine alone. The delicate table centerpiece is of Meissen porcelain.

Small Gallery of Mirrors

The Small Gallery of Mirrors was constructed in memory of the (no longer existing) "Petite Galerie" in Versailles. It is 20 m long and adjoins two angled rooms, one at each end. Placed in the niches are statues of the 4 continents by Johann Hirt. Cupids and genii, allegories of art and science, and a series of figures from Greek mythology (in the ceiling painting by Josef Munch) populate this deceptively large hall. Light is provided by the gilded bronze candelabras on the tables in front of the mirrors and the 5 crystal chandeliers hanging from the ceiling.

Bathroom

From his bedroom, Ludwig could reach the surprisingly modern bathroom by means of a spiral staircase. The bathroom is on the ground floor with an oval pool of marble and marble steps leading down into it. The surrounding walls offer a mediterranean panorama painted by Josef Weisser. Venus, the Roman godess of Love, enjoys herself with her attendants.

Dressing Room

The Rose Cabinet adjoining the bathroom functions as the Dressing Room. It is in fact a 2nd mirror room, with endless reflections of the carvings creating the impression of a tangle of golden branches within the room.

Scenes of the Bath of Diana and the Bath of Venus above the doors, and Neptune and Amphitrite on the ceiling were copied from François Boucher's paintings by Josef Weisser. Delicate chandeliers and pink draperies and upholstery complete the decor of this charming room.

Ludwig II Museum

**Audience Chamber
from the Residence**

Forty years after the death of Ludwig II, this museum was opened in Herrenchiemsee, and in 1986, after some alterations, it was opened again to the public.

The museum contains artifacts that recall the life and work of the "Fairytale King". Personal items and documents, photographs and paintings, Ludwig's christening gown, his death mask, and also origi-

nal scores to some of Wagner's operas plus some valuable articles from his estate, ensure that the memory of Ludwig will be perpetuated.

The most impressive pieces of the collection come from the Royal Apartments of the Residence in Munich, for example the opulent throne from the Audience Chamber designed by Franz Seitz between 1867 and 1869. The throne is complete with gilded carvings of trumpet-blowing genii.

First Bedroom
from Linderhof Castle

Fortunately the first bedroom of Linderhof has survived and it shows the coming together of the elegant lines of the French style and the sweeping arabesques of the Bavarian Rococo. Golden angels at the foot of the canopy bed watch over a myriad of richly ornamented shells and leaves.

Dining Room and Bedroom
from the Residence

Parts of the Royal bedroom of the Munich residence that survived the 2nd World War are kept in this museum, and include the royal-blue velvet canopy of the bed, with fine embroidery in golden thread, and a copy of Raffael's "Madonna della Sedia" (from the Pitti Palace in Florence) by Tito Berti, completed in 1857.

Items from the Dining-Room designed by Franz Seitz include the heavy, gilded dining table and chairs. The chair with arms reserved for the King holds a medallion with the King's monogram and crown.

Winter Garden

One of the most expensive and fascinating creations of the Residence – Ludwig's Winter Garden – is brought again to life through a series of original artifacts and brilliant photographs by the royal photographer Josef Albert. The garden's plans were drawn by Carl von Effner, and include almost everything that the royal imagination could dream of in creating this enchanting retreat: caves with stalactites; waterfalls; an Indian fishing hut and a Moorish kiosk; exotic vegetation; paths and waterways; a boat; some swans - and a fantastic landscape projection, all crowned by a most subtle illumination.

Schachen Hunting Lodge

The Schachen Hunting Lodge is situated over 1800 m high in the Wetterstein mountains south of Garmisch-Partenkirchen. The simple wooden exterior belies the oriental interior of overwhelming magnificence.

The lodge was created by Georg Schneider. In the center stands a bubbling Moorish fountain; colourful silk divans and inlaid smoking tables lines the walls, and the room is exotically illuminated through stained glass windows.